cat
katt

rabbit

kanin

dog

hund

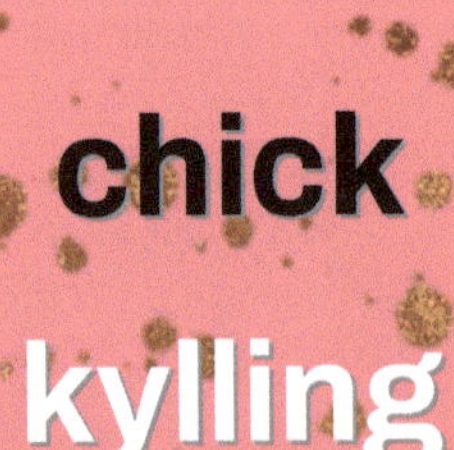

chick

kylling

duck
and

sheep

sau

goat

geit

pig

gris

donkey

esel

horse

hest

cow

ku

mouse

mus

bat

flaggermus

bee

bie

spider

edderkopp

fox

rev

deer

hjort

squirrel

ekorn

hedgehog

pinnsvin

owl

ugle

frog

frosk

snake

slange

racoon

vaskebjørn

parrot

papegøye

toucan

tukan

alligator

alligator

sea turtle

sjøskilpadde

flamingo

flamingo

penguin

pingvin

crab

krabbe

jellyfish

manet

seal

sel

shark

hai

whale

hval

orca

spekkhogger

starfish
sjøstjerne

rhinoceros

neshorn

panda

panda

monkey

ape

lion

løve

tiger

tiger

elephant

elefant